S0-BDO-812

BASIC
HEREDITY

Table of Contents

Introduction

Have you ever wondered why you look the way you do? Maybe your nose looks like your grandmother's nose. Maybe your eyes are the same shape as your father's eyes. Have you seen brothers and sisters who look like each other? How does this happen?

To answer those questions and more, scientists study basic **heredity** (huh-REH-dih-tee). Heredity is the passing of traits controlled by genes from generation to generation. You are, in large part, a product of your **genes**. Genes are passed down from parents to children. Genes determine how you look and the way you grow. Genes also play a role in how a person acts. They can affect how healthy a person will be.

▲ Family members often look like each other. This is because they share some of the same genes.

Scientists are trying to learn more about genes. To do this, they study genes in the laboratory. They try to find out what makes up each gene. Scientists want to know what trait each gene controls. By understanding genes, they can learn the secrets of how genes work. Maybe then they could control genes. They could cure diseases caused by faulty genes.

You are born with your genes. It is important to understand just what your genes can and cannot do. What do genes mean to your health, your personality, and your appearance? Read on to discover how you got the genes you have.

Scientists study ▶ genes in laboratories. They hope to be able to cure faulty genes someday.

Understanding Heredity

You are who you are—and not a turtle, for example—because of DNA. DNA is **deoxyribonucleic acid** (dee-AHK-see-RY-boh-noo-KLAY-ik A-sid). It is a code that contains all the genetic information of a cell. The DNA code tells each part of a cell how to grow. The code tells human cells to grow into humans and turtle cells to grow into turtles.

A DNA strand is shaped like a double helix. A helix is a spiral shape. DNA looks like a twisting rope ladder. There are four different bases that make up the steps of the ladder. A base is a type of chemical. One is A for adenine (A-duh-neen). Another is T for thymine (THY-meen). C stands for cytosine (SY-toh-seen). The last one is G for guanine (GWAH-neen).

D
P

Thymine
Adenine
Guanine
Cytosine
D = Deoxyribose (sugar)
P = Phosphate
o = Hydrogen Bond

▲ DNA strand

They Made a Difference

In 1953, James Watson and Francis Crick discovered that DNA was shaped like a double helix. Pictures created by chemist Rosalind Franklin helped. She used x-rays to create images of DNA. These images helped Watson and Crick discover the structure of the DNA molecule.

The bases always form the same pairs. This is because they are chemically attracted to each other. The C and G form a pair. The A and T make up the other pair. These **base pairs** form the alphabet of our DNA. The order of the bases is very important. Different orders are called sequences. Sequences of the base pairs write our DNA "book." Each combination is a code. It gives the cell instructions about how to function. How can just four bases produce so many different traits? There are about three billion pairs of bases in the human **genome** (JEE-nome). The sum total of DNA in a living thing is called its genome. That's a lot of possible combinations. If you typed all the base sequences of a person's DNA, the stacked paper would be higher than the Empire State Building!

When it comes to DNA, it's not the size that matters. More complex organisms do not necessarily have more DNA. In fact, salamanders, Easter lilies, and lungfish all have more DNA than humans! Every living thing has its own genome.

1. Solve This

A gene contains 65 base pairs. Of those, 20 are pairs of A and T bases. What percentage of the gene is made up of C and G base pairs?

Math ✔ Point

Could you solve this problem without knowing that there are 20 A-T base pairs?

Genes

DNA is the code of life. So, where do genes fit in? Genes are made of long segments of DNA, like beads on a string.

Not all genes are the same size. They contain different lengths of DNA. The gene that controls insulin is a shorter gene. Insulin controls the intake and use of sugar in cells. The gene is about 1,700 base pairs long. The longest known gene has more than two million base pairs. Problems with this gene may cause muscle diseases.

Scientists consider a gene to be the basic unit of heredity. It's a tiny part of a cell with a big job to do. Each gene is responsible for a certain trait. These include height, hair, or eye color.

The gene does its job by telling the cell how to make proteins. Proteins are involved in almost every function of our body. Some proteins help grow hair and nails. Other proteins are involved with the process of digestion. Different genes contain instructions for making different proteins.

Scientists have ▶ found the gene that controls insulin. This is a computerized image of the gene.

Insulin (Chain A and B) molecule 1
Insulin (Chain A and B) molecule 1
Zinc ions

Chromosomes

Genes are on **chromosomes** (KROH-muh-somez), which are structures in the nucleus of a cell. Chromosomes carry genetic information. They pass on genes to the next generation when the cell divides.

Chromosomes usually come in pairs. Each kind of living thing usually has the same number of chromosomes. Humans have forty-six chromosomes in twenty-three chromosomal pairs.

Researchers have mapped the entire human genome. They can find where each gene is located on a specific chromosome.

✓ POINT

Talk About It

Review the information you've read so far. Then tell a partner the relationship among DNA, genes, and chromosomes.

2. Solve This

Scientists use special language to describe a certain gene's location. For example, the APOE gene, responsible for processing fats, is on chromosome 19. It starts with base pair number 50,100,901 and ends with base pair number 50,104,488. How many base pairs does this gene contain?

Math ✓ Point

Do you think the APOE gene is considered a long, medium, or short gene? Why?

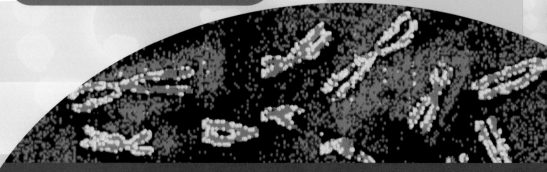

▲ Human chromosomes look like small, crooked sticks.

Mitosis and Meiosis

The human body has about 100 trillion cells. Eventually, some of these cells will become damaged and die. The body creates new cells to replace them. A cell divides itself into two exact copies. This process is called mitosis (my-TOH-sis). Millions of cells in the human body divide each second.

Passing genetic information to the new cell is part of mitosis. The new cell could not survive without the DNA code. Each time a cell divides, the chromosomes make an exact copy of themselves. These copies are passed to the new cells. That way, each cell will contain genes. The genes will make the proteins the body needs.

But how did you get your genes in the first place? You received half of your genes from your father. You received half from your mother. This happened because special reproductive cells in the body divide twice. This process is called meiosis (my-OH-sis).

mitosis ▶

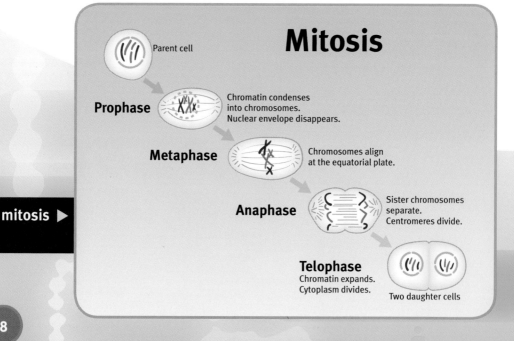

Mitosis

Parent cell

Prophase — Chromatin condenses into chromosomes. Nuclear envelope disappears.

Metaphase — Chromosomes align at the equatorial plate.

Anaphase — Sister chromosomes separate. Centromeres divide.

Telophase — Chromatin expands. Cytoplasm divides.

Two daughter cells

First, all the chromosomes in the reproductive cells duplicate. They create two cells as they do in mitosis. But then, the cells duplicate again. This reduces their number of chromosomes by half. Now there are four new cells. Each has only twenty-three chromosomes.

During meiosis, the chromosomes line up in pairs. Sometimes genes jump from chromosome to chromosome. This process is called crossing-over. The two chromosome pairs trade genes. Some of the father's genes jump to the mother's chromosome. Some of the mother's genes jump to the father's chromosome. Crossing-over mixes the genes. It helps create more variety of traits among a couple's children.

Each female egg cell has twenty-three chromosomes. So does each male sperm cell. These cells join during reproduction. The new cell they create will have forty-six chromosomes. Half will be from each parent.

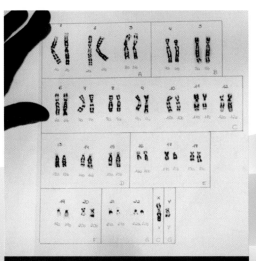

▲ Scientists have given each chromosome pair a number. This helps them locate genes.

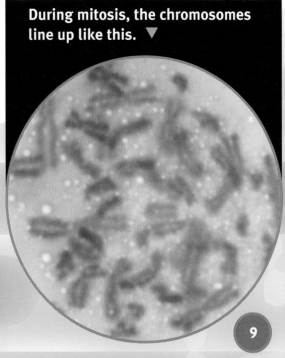

During mitosis, the chromosomes line up like this. ▼

Traits

Each child inherits a unique set of chromosomes. This means that each child will have his or her own set of traits. A trait is a specific quality or feature. So what are some traits you can inherit?

The most obvious traits are physical. These traits determine how someone looks. The size of your feet, the color of your hair, the shape of your lips, and the color of your skin are traits.

Behavioral traits are not as obvious. These affect how someone acts. Maybe you inherited a sense of humor like your mother's. Perhaps you're easily startled like your father. Do you have a quick temper like your aunt? These would be examples of your genes influencing the way you behave.

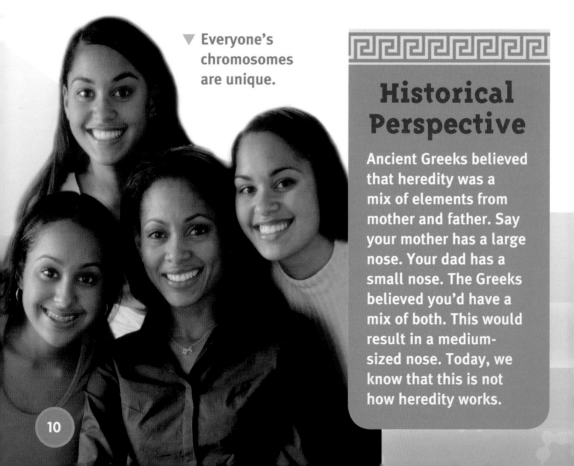

▼ Everyone's chromosomes are unique.

Historical Perspective

Ancient Greeks believed that heredity was a mix of elements from mother and father. Say your mother has a large nose. Your dad has a small nose. The Greeks believed you'd have a mix of both. This would result in a medium-sized nose. Today, we know that this is not how heredity works.

There are some traits that you cannot see. An increased chance of getting a certain disease is one of these. Scientists have found genetic links to heart disease, obesity, and certain kinds of cancer. Some mental illnesses may also run in a family. For example, some people inherit a greater risk of developing depression.

3. Solve This

The Greeks believed that a child inherits an exact combination of both the mother's and father's traits. A mother was 5 feet (152 centimeters) tall. A father was 5 feet, 6 inches (168 centimeters) tall. How tall would their child grow up to be based on this theory?

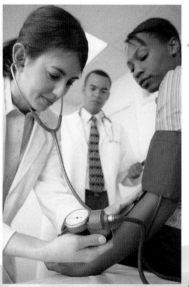

◀ The doctor is checking this person's blood pressure. High blood pressure can be inherited.

Math ✔ Point

What do you need to know about inches and feet to solve this problem?

Parents may pass on genes that make it more likely that their children will gain weight. ▶

Chapter 2

Why Do You Look Like You Do?

Genes are the blueprint, or plan, for making each living thing. They affect everything, including gender. You are the gender you are because of your chromosomes.

Genes on the twenty-third chromosome pair determine whether a child will be male or female. The female chromosome is called X. The male chromosome is called Y. A child always inherits an X chromosome from the mother. If a child inherits an X chromosome from the father, this child will be female. On the other hand, if a child inherits a Y chromosome from the father, this child will be male.

Sometimes the X and Y pair do not produce a male. One example is a Spanish athlete named Maria Patino, who runs hurdles. She carries an X and Y chromosome. But she had a **mutation** (myoo-TAY-shun) in one of her genes. A mutation is a change in the gene. This caused her to develop genetically into a woman instead of a man. Because of her mutation, she has the body of a woman.

Sex Determination From Male & Female Chromosomes

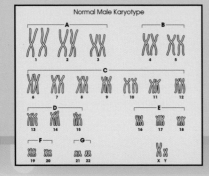

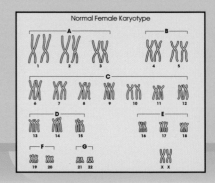

Normally, no one would have ever known about Maria's mutation. However, sports authorities do genetic testing. They make sure people are the gender that they claim. This ensures that a man can't disguise himself and compete against females. Maria was tested before a race in 1985. She did not test as a woman, and she wasn't allowed to compete.

Maria fought this decision. A geneticist explained her condition to the sports authorities. The geneticist said that Maria did not have an unfair advantage of muscle strength over other women. As a result, Maria was allowed to compete again. She participated in the 1992 Olympic Games in Barcelona.

▲ Maria Patino (left) was allowed to compete against other female athletes in the 1992 Olympics.

 **Careers**

Bioethicist

A bioethicist studies science and ethics. Ethics is a set of principles of proper conduct. On the job, a bioethicist specializes in controversial issues. Controversial means that many people disagree about the topic.

A bioethicist tries to determine good guidelines for research. This is important in controversial fields, such as genetic engineering. This branch of genetics involves changing people's genes to create desired traits.

13

Reproductive chromosomes can also influence how traits are passed down to children. Females inherit two X chromosomes. These are similar in size. Most of the genes show up in pairs. Sometimes a gene on one of the X chromosomes is faulty. Then, the gene on the other usually will perform the function. This helps prevent disorders.

Men inherit an X and a Y chromosome. Many of the genes on the X chromosome are not on the Y. A gene found only on the X chromosome is called a sex-linked trait.

Let's say a gene on the X is faulty. There is usually no other gene on the Y to make up for it. This makes it more likely for certain genetic disorders to develop in men. Red-green color-blindness is a common sex-linked disorder. It affects men more often than women.

They Made a Difference

Researcher Barbara McClintock discovered that genes jump from place to place on chromosomes, causing different things, such as the varying colors and spots on corn. In 1983, she became the first female recipient of the Nobel Prize for Physiology (medicine) who did not share the honor with a male counterpart.

▲ Baldness is a sex-linked trait. It is passed down on the X chromosome and usually affects men more than women.

Parents can pass down mutations to their children. Oddly, a mutation can result in one disease if inherited from the mother, and another disease if inherited from the father. This is called **imprinting**.

A mutated gene on chromosome 15 can cause two different diseases. If the mutation is from the mother, the child develops Angelman's syndrome.

A child with this disorder will lack normal mental development and have seizures. If the mutation is from the father, the child develops Prader-Willi syndrome. A child with this disorder lacks normal mental development and becomes very overweight.

▼ **Oncogenes are genes in a cancer cell.**

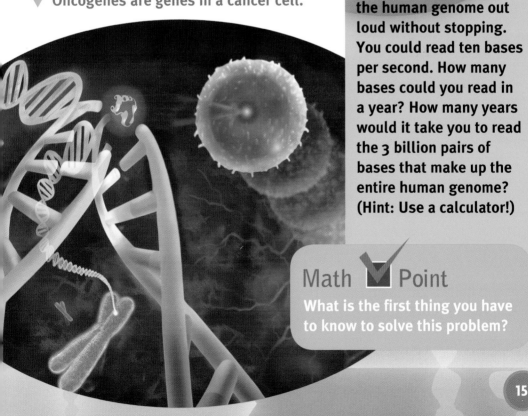

4. Solve This

Say you read the base sequences that make up the human genome out loud without stopping. You could read ten bases per second. How many bases could you read in a year? How many years would it take you to read the 3 billion pairs of bases that make up the entire human genome? (Hint: Use a calculator!)

Math ✔ Point

What is the first thing you have to know to solve this problem?

Genotype and Phenotype

Did you know that you have a lot in common with a mouse? Mice share about ninety percent of our genetic material. Look around you. You probably see many people who look different than you do. But you have many things in common. All human beings share 99.9 percent of the same genetic material.

The **genotype** (JEE-noh-tipe) is the actual genetic makeup of an organism. But the **phenotype** (FEE-noh-tipe) is much different. A phenotype is the observable physical traits of a living thing. Most people differ from each other by only 0.01 percent. Yet almost every person has a unique appearance.

It's a Fact

If unraveled, DNA in one human cell would stretch in a straight line for more than 6 feet (2 meters).

Everyone's ▶ genetic makeup is similar, yet we all look very different.

The exception to this is identical twins. They share the same phenotype. Identical twins form when a fertilized egg cell divides. Each copy has identical genetic information. And each develops into a baby.

Fingerprints are one way to tell identical twins apart. The fingerprints of identical twins are somewhat alike. Even so, fingerprint experts can tell the difference.

Scientists are not sure if the differences are genetic. Some scientists think that the environment makes the fingerprints different. For example, the things twins touch on a daily basis could wear down the skin differently.

Humans share genetic material with different organisms.

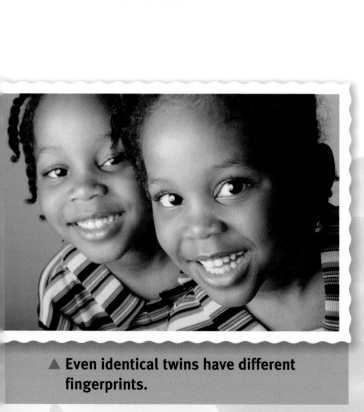

▲ Even identical twins have different fingerprints.

Laws of Heredity

An Austrian monk named Gregor Mendel studied heredity. While he worked in the garden of his monastery, Mendel studied the plants. He experimented with more than 28,000 pea plants. He discovered how traits were passed down from parents to children.

Mendel focused his research on seven traits of pea plants. These included height and seed color. He fertilized plants with different traits and recorded the results.

Mendel found that two short plants always produced a new short plant. However, a tall plant and a short plant produced a tall plant. In later generations, three of the plants would be tall and one would be short.

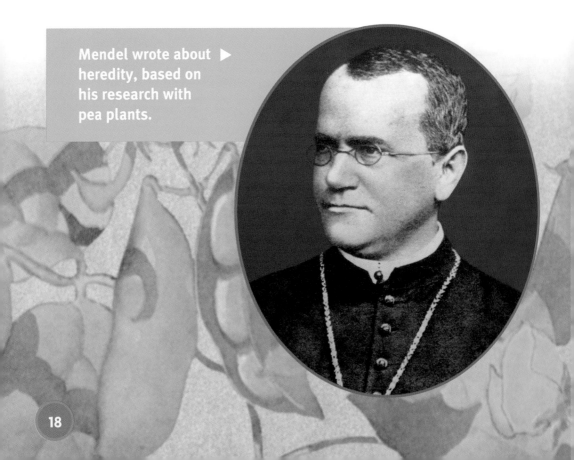

Mendel wrote about ▶ heredity, based on his research with pea plants.

The research led Mendel to develop the laws of heredity. Scientists still use these laws today:

- **Alleles** (uh-LEELZ) are the different forms that genes can take. These are traits such as short or tall.
- Each physical trait comes from one allele.
- Alleles come in pairs. People carry two genes for each trait.
- The next generation receives only one of each pair from its parent.
- There is an equal chance that either allele will be passed down.
- Finally, some alleles are **dominant**. Others are **recessive**.

5. Solve This

A couple has a 25% chance of having a child with curly hair and a 50% chance of having a child with blue eyes. What are the chances they will have a child with curly hair AND blue eyes?

Math Point

What steps did you take to get your answer?

Mendel's experiments showed that alleles are different variations of the same gene. There are usually at least two alleles responsible for each trait. They're found on the same spot on each chromosome in a pair.

Sometimes alleles share the same code for a trait. Then, the trait will always be expressed. Let's look at the alleles that contain the codes for your eye color. Maybe you have two alleles for blue eyes. Then, you will have blue eyes. Maybe you have two alleles for brown eyes. Then, you'll have brown eyes.

Other times you may inherit two different alleles. Maybe you have an allele for brown eyes from your father. You might have an allele for blue eyes from your mother. If this happens, which trait is expressed?

The trait depends on which alleles are dominant or recessive. Dominant alleles always express their trait. They mask the recessive allele. For example, the allele for brown eyes is dominant. It will be expressed even if you have an allele for blue eyes.

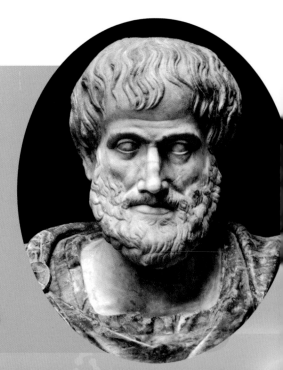

It's a Fact

Famous Greek philosopher Aristotle studied heredity. He believed that parents' interaction with nature affected their children's appearances. For example, let's say a mother broke her arm. Then, her future child would have a weak or underdeveloped bone in that arm.

The blue-eye allele is still part of your genotype. So, you could pass on a copy of it to your children. But blue eyes won't show up on your phenotype. This is because the code is overridden by the brown-eye allele. In order to have blue eyes, you'd have to inherit blue-eye alleles from both your mother and father.

Sometimes neither gene is dominant. If this happens, both traits may be expressed. This creates a blended phenotype. For example, a red carnation and a white carnation produce pink carnation offspring. In people, this can sometimes happen with eye color. Neither the allele for blue or green eyes is dominant. Someone may inherit one blue allele and one green allele. Then, their eye color might be hazel.

Everyday Science

Look at the people around you. Their appearance is mostly a result of their genes. Gather a group of friends together. Make a table of their traits. Write down each friend's name. Read the list of dominant and recessive traits. Use it to record the dominant and recessive traits in you and your friends. Can you figure out your friends' genotypes from their recessive traits?

▲ Having freckles is a dominant trait.

Your Genes or Your Environment?

Scientists have long debated whether genes or our environment are more important. The answer is still unknown. But today, most scientists agree that both are important. Often our personal experiences and our genetic makeup interact. The interaction can affect how we look and act.

Take your physical traits. Perhaps you inherited a gene that makes it likely that you'll gain weight. You can alter your environment. You can exercise and eat healthful foods. This will help you stay fit. You can study and develop your mind. This might raise your I.Q., or intelligence quotient.

Environment is part of who ▼ you are. If you study hard, you might raise your I.Q.

Genes play a role in a person's health just as the environment does. You may inherit faulty genes or chromosomes from your parents. This causes genetic disorders that can seriously affect your quality of life. One such genetic condition is albinism. People with albinism have no pigment in their hair, skin, or eyes.

Certain diseases can run in a family. People inherit susceptibility (suh-sep-tih-BIH-lih-tee) genes from their parents. But researchers don't know how or why yet.

Susceptibility genes increase the risk of developing diseases. You may have one or more of these genes. This doesn't mean you will get the disease. Many factors are involved. These include environment and lifestyle choices as well as genes.

6. Solve This

Each year, one out of every 17,000 people is born with albinism. If 1.3 million people are born in a year, how many of them can you expect to have albinism?

Math ✔ Point

Explain how you solved the problem.

▲ People with albinism cannot adapt to bright sun. Too much sun could cause serious injury.

Genes play a role in your body type and athletic ability. Genes partly determine height, muscle size, and strength. Some people are luckier than others in the genetic lottery. Famous athletes may have certain physical traits that help increase the likelihood that they will excel at a given sport. However, their passion to play, practice, compete, and hone their skills for, say, baseball over football, or skiing over surfing, is influenced by many factors, such as the geography, the culture, or even the family that they grow up in.

Researchers believe they've found the gene that separates good athletes from great athletes. The gene is called ACTN3.

The ACTN3 gene is something we are all born with, so to a degree we are all athletes. Each person has two copies of it: one from each parent.

Genes determine ▶ how tall you will be. Genes also affect your dexterity. Dexterity is skill in using your hands.

This gene is responsible for making a special protein that assists the body in its ability to contract muscles at high velocities. This allows people with the ACTN3 gene to more easily succeed at fast-spaced sports such as sprinting, where athletes need explosive power.

In some people, a variant prevents the gene from making this protein. These people tend to be good at endurance sports such as distance running, swimming, or cross-country skiing. Athletes who got the variant from only one parent may be suited for both endurance and sprint-power sports. However, most scientists agree that most athletes become champion athletes because of a combination of factors, including genetic makeup, environment, and lifestyle choices.

7. Solve This

Most adults have a resting heart rate that averages about 80 beats per minute. Trained athletes have a significantly lower resting heart rate, usually averaging about 50 bpm, indicating better overall heart function and cardiovascular fitness. How many more times in 3 hours will the average adult's heart beat compared with that of a professionally trained athlete?

Math ✔ Point

What do you need to know about time to help you solve this problem?

▲ Greg LeMond won the Tour de France three times. He owes his success to his genetic strength and lifestyle choices.

Behavioral Genetics

Genes also play a role in behavior. Behavioral **genetics** is the study of the relationship between genes and personality. The exact part genes play is still unknown. Scientists try to find genes that affect how a person acts.

Scientists study behavior and genetics. To do this, some conduct research studies with twins. Researcher Thomas Bouchard studied twins. He examined the behavior of identical twins who were separated at birth. The twins shared the same genetic material, but they were raised in different homes. If genes shaped behavior, both twins should have common traits. It shouldn't matter what the environment was.

"In Their Own Words"

John B. Watson was a scientist who believed the environment influenced personality and behavior more than heredity.

"Give me a dozen healthy infants and my own specific world to bring them up in, and I'll guarantee to take any one at random and train him to become any type of specialist I might select . . . regardless of . . . his ancestors."

Bouchard found that quite a few twins did share many common traits. One example is Oskar Stohr and Jack Yufe. The twin brothers were raised by different families.

Bouchard arranged a meeting for the twins. They both arrived wearing similar clothes and glasses. They even had the same style of mustache. Both men liked to play jokes on other people. One of their jokes was sneezing loudly in elevators.

Recently, researchers have found new genes. They think the genes affect personality traits, including memory and a tendency toward violence. Other scientists disagree with the findings. They say that each behavior is complicated. They believe that behavior involves the interaction of many different genes.

It's a Fact

Identical twins Jim Lewis and Jim Springer met at age 39 during Bouchard's study. They both had been married two times. Each twin's wives were named Linda and Betty. Their dogs were named Toy. And their sons' names were James Alan and James Allen.

Twins are very much alike, even when they do not grow up together.

Conclusion

Heredity is an important science. It helps us understand how humans pass down traits to future generations. You inherited half of your genes from your mother. The other half came from your father. You will pass on half of your genetic material to your children.

Genes are on chromosomes in your cells. Genes are made up of DNA. This code tells your cells how to grow. It tells a cell how to make proteins.

Proteins are necessary to make the body function well.

Each gene is responsible for one or more traits. These include physical traits that determine how you look. Behavioral traits affect how you act. Genes that come in pairs and determine traits are called alleles. Some alleles are dominant. Others are recessive. Dominant genes are always expressed.

☑ POINT

Read More About It

In Basic Heredity, you've read about scientists, doctors, bioethicists, researchers, geneticists, and genetic engineers. Ask your teacher or librarian to help you find books and Internet sites about the career you find most interesting.

◄ Scientists have figured out the sequence of DNA. This will help them understand our genes.

Both your environment and your genes play a role in who you are today.

Knowing about your genes can help improve your well-being. Maybe you have susceptibility genes for a certain disease. You can live a healthy lifestyle to help control the risks. You can't change your genes. You can learn to live with them in the best way possible.

Major Discoveries in Heredity

186: Gregor Mendel publishes a paper, "Experiments on Plant Hybridization," about the results of his pea plant experiments.

1903: Scientist Walter S. Sutton demonstrates that chromosomes are the cell parts that contain hereditary material.

1910: Thomas Hunt Morgan proves that genes are on chromosomes.

193: Barbara McClintock and Harriet Creighton establish that chromosomes form the basis of genetics.

194: Edward Lawrie Tatum and George Wells Beadle discover that genes contain instructions for making certain proteins.

1944: Scientists find that DNA is genetic material.

195: Scientists prove that DNA is the genetic information of all organisms, including people.

1953: Scientists discover that a DNA molecule is shaped like a double helix.

1956: Scientists find out that the correct chromosome number in humans is forty-six.

1999: The first human gene is sequenced.

2003: The Human Genome Project is completed. It sequenced 99 percent of the human genome with 99.99 percent accuracy.

Solve This Answers

1 Page 5 **69 percent**
65 – 20 = 45 C and G base pairs
45/65 = .69 or 69%

2 Page 7 **3,587 base pairs long**
50,104,488 – 50,100,901 =
3,587

3 Page 11 **5 feet, 3 inches
(160 centimeters) tall**
5 feet + 5 feet, 6 inches =
10 feet, 6 inches
(152 cm + 168 cm = 320 cm)
10 feet, 6 inches = 126 inches
Half of 126 inches is 63
inches, or 5 feet, 3 inches.
(Half of 320 cm is 160 cm.)

4 Page 15 **315,360,000 base
pairs in a year; 9.5 years to
read the 3 billion pairs**
10/second x 60 = 600/minute
600 x 60 = 36,000/hour
36,000 x 24 = 864,000/day
864,000 x 365 =
315,360,000/year
3,000,000,000/315,360,000 =
9.5 years

5 Page 19 **12.5% chance**
.25 x .50 or 1/4 x 1/2 = 1/8
or 0.125

6 Page 23 **about 76 people
would have albinism**
1.3 million = 1,300,000
1,300,000/17,000 = 76.5

7 Page 25 **5,400 more beats
during a 3-hour time span**
80 – 50 = 30 more beats per
minute
30 x 60 = 1,800 more beats
per hour
1,800 x 3 = 5,400 more beats
during a 3-hour time span

Glossary

allele — (uh-LEEL) one of several forms a gene can take (page 19)

base pair — (BAYS PAIR) two bases that bond together to form one rung on the DNA molecule (page 5)

chromosome — (KROH-muh-some) the rod-like structure in the cell's nucleus that contains genes (page 7)

deoxyribonucleic acid (DNA) — (dee-AHK-see-RY-boh-noo-KLAY-ik A-sid) the chemical that contains an organism's genetic code (page 4)

dominant — (DAH-mih-nunt) an allele with a trait that is always expressed (page 19)

gene — (JEEN) part of DNA; a segment of DNA that holds the instructions for making one or more proteins (page 2)

genetics — (jeh-NEH-tiks) the study of genes and heredity (page 26)

genome — (JEE-nome) the complete genetic information of a living being (page 5)

genotype — (JEE-noh-tipe) the actual genetic makeup of an organism (page 16)

heredity — (huh-REH-dih-tee) the passing of genes and characteristics from parents to their children (page 2)

imprinting — (im-PRINT-ing) the way a mutation in genes can cause one disease if passed down from the father and another disease if passed down from the mother (page 15)

mutation — (myoo-TAY-shun) a random change in one or more base pairs (page 12)

phenotype — (FEE-noh-tipe) the observable display of a trait in a living thing (page 16)

recessive — (rih-SEH-siv) an allele that expresses its trait in the next generation only if there are two copies (page 19)

31

Index